MAPS AND MAPPING

BARBARA TAYLOR

Kingfisher Books

NEW YORK

KINGFISHER
Larousse Kingfisher Chambers Inc.
95 Madison Avenue
New York, New York 10016

First American edition 1993
10 9 8 7 6 5 (PB)
10 9 8 7 6 5 4 3 (HC)
10 9 8 7 6 5 4 3 2 (LIB. BDG.)
© Grisewood & Dempsey Ltd. 1992

Library of Congress
Cataloging-in-Publication Data
Taylor, Barbara
   Maps and mapping / Barbara Taylor. —
1st American ed.
   p. cm. — (Young Discoverers)
   Includes index.
Summary: Explains what maps are and why
they are used, introduces symbols found on
maps, and describes how cartographers map
the world. Includes related activities.
   1. Maps—Juvenile literature. [1. Maps.]
I. Title. II. Series: Taylor, Barbara. Young
discoverers.
GA105.6.T39 1993
912—dc20 92-23373 CIP AC

ISBN 1-85697-863-X (HC)
ISBN 1-85697-936-9 (PB)
ISBN 1-85697-628-9 (LIB. BDG.)

Series editor: Sue Nicholson
Series and cover design: Terry Woodley
Design: Ben White
Picture research: Elaine Willis
Illustrations: Kuo Kang Chen pp.2, 10, 11 (top
   right), 15, 18-19, 20 (bottom), 21, 23; Chris
   Forsey pp.8, 16 (top), 17 bottom right), 31;
   Hayward Art Group pp.26, 28-29; Kevin
   Maddison pp. 6 (top right), 7, 13, 14, 20 (top),
   21, 22 (bottom), 27 (top), 30 (top); Maltings
   Partnership pp.8-9 (bottom), 12, 22 (top); Janos
   Marphy, Kathy Jakeman Illustration pp.5 (top
   right), 11 (bottom left), 12 (top right), 16-17,
   24-25, 27 (bottom), 28 (top); Simon Tegg, Simon
   Girling & Associates pp.4-5, 6 (bottom)
Cover illustration: Kevin Maddison
Photographs: British Library p.25; Earth Satellite
   Corporation/Science Photo Library p.22;
   Marconi Underwater Systems p.13; NASA
   pp.24, 30; Christine Osbourne Pictures p.21

Printed in Spain

About This Book

This book tells you about different kinds of maps – how they are drawn, how they are used, and how to understand them. It also has lots of ideas for projects and things to look out for. You should be able to find nearly everything you need to do the projects around your home. You may need to buy some items, but they are all cheap and easy to find. Sometimes you will need to ask an adult to help you, such as when using a map on a hike in the countryside.

Activity Hints

● Before you begin, read the instructions carefully and collect all the things that you will need.

● When you have finished, clear everything away, especially sharp things like knives and scissors.

● Start a special notebook. Keep a record of what you do in each project and the things you find out.

Contents

Make your own Treasure Island map – see page 23.

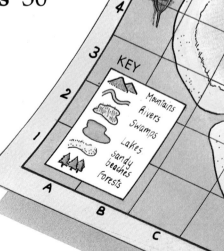

A Bird's Eye View

Have you ever used a map? Maps can help us find our way to a place even if we have never been there before. Most maps are flat drawings of a piece of the Earth's surface seen from above – the sort of view that birds have when they fly overhead. A map is easier to use than written instructions because it is a simple picture showing where things are. Ancient maps were drawn on animal skins or cloth, and the word "map" comes from the Latin word *mappa*, meaning cloth.

The map below is a plan of the ground shown in the picture, as seen by the bird flying above. The map shows the buildings, roads, trees, and pond. Maps only show things that are always there. They do not show cars or people.

When they draw maps, mapmakers must decide what to put in and what to leave out, depending on who will use the map and why they need it.

👁 Eye-Spy

These objects have all been drawn from above. Can you see what they are? Draw other things from above and have a guessing game with a friend.

5

Mapping Your Room

The best way to understand how maps work and how useful they can be is to draw one yourself. Choose a small area to start with, like your bedroom. Before you start, decide how big you want your map to be. You will not have room to include everything on your map, just the most important things like your furniture and the door and window. The first thing to do is to find out the exact size of your room and the position of the things in it. The project on the opposite page will show you how to do this.

You will often see large maps like this one in parks. They usually have an arrow or a circle to show you exactly where you are.

My House to Yours

Has anyone ever asked you how to get from one place to another?

Close your eyes and imagine the route you usually take from your house to your friend's house, or try to describe the route shown on this map. Could you give directions so that a stranger could follow them? It's not as easy as it sounds! You need to remember all the important landmarks, like churches or certain stores, and you must say exactly when to turn right or left.

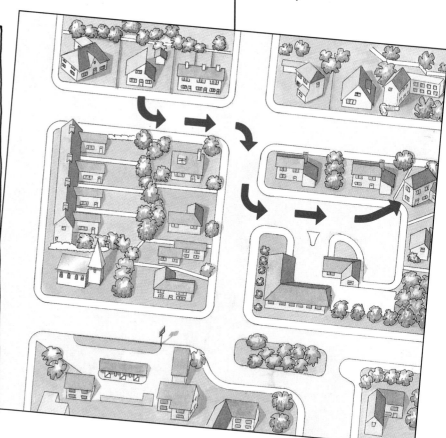

6

Do it yourself

To make an accurate map of your room, you need some large-squared graph paper, a ruler, and a sharp pencil.

More Things to Try

Make another plan to show your furniture in new places. This is a good way of testing whether your bed will fit somewhere else without moving it around! Try making a plan of another room in your house.

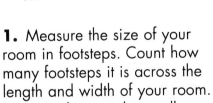

Bed

Bedside Cupboard

Window

Chest of drawers

Desk

Chair

Door

16 squares

21 squares

1. Measure the size of your room in footsteps. Count how many footsteps it is across the length and width of your room.

Remember to take small steps so that the heel of one foot touches the toe of the other. In this way, all your steps will be the same size so your measurements will be more accurate.

2. Imagine that one of your footsteps is equal to one square on the graph paper, then draw in the edges of your room. For example, if your room is 21 steps long and 16 steps wide, draw a box on your paper that is 21 squares long and 16 squares wide.

3. Mark in the position of your door and window. Now measure around your large pieces of furniture in footsteps. Then, using your ruler, draw them in the correct position on your plan.

Map Scales

On most maps, everything is shrunk, or scaled down, by the same amount. So on the map of your room, one footstep equaled one square on your paper. You could also have made up a scale in which one foot of your room was equal to half an inch on your map. Map scales compare the size of the map with the real size of a place. Maps can be drawn to any scale. Look at the four maps below. Each shows Florence, a city in Italy, but each map is at a different scale.

These toy cars are 25 times smaller than real cars. In a similar way, maps are drawn to a much smaller scale than the real places they show.

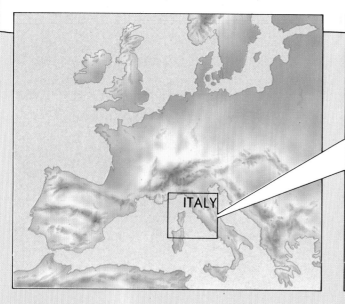

ITALY

On this scale of map, 1 inch equals 600 miles. There are about 38,000,000 inches in 600 miles, so the scale is written as 1:38,000,000.

0   375 km*

0   600
miles

ITALY

This scale of map shows where Florence is in Italy. As 1 inch on the map equals 100 miles on the ground, the scale is 1:6,300,000.

0   60 km

0   100
miles

* Some countries measure in centimeters and kilometers while others use inches and miles. The top scale shows the number of kilometers represented by 1 centimeter on the map.

Railroad Maps

Some maps are not drawn to scale. Instead they are distorted, or changed, to make them easier to understand. For example, on this map of the railroad system in Tokyo, the tracks are drawn as straight lines with plenty of space between the stations. In real life, the lines criss-cross the city like a maze so an accurate map would be too confusing.

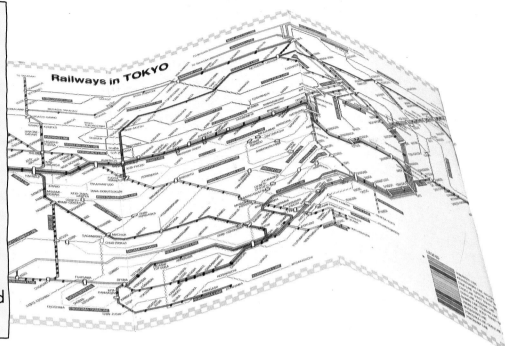

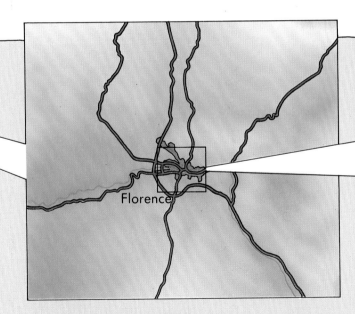

This is a more detailed map that shows only Florence with its roads and rivers. Here, 1 inch equals 16 miles, so the scale is 1:1,000,000.

0   10 km

0   16
miles

This is the most detailed map of Florence. It shows just part of the city. Here, 1 inch equals 1.6 miles so the scale is written as 1:100,000.

0   1 km

0   1.6
miles

9

Do it yourself

To understand how scale works, try drawing a "map" of this book.

1. Draw around the book on a large sheet of paper and measure the outline. The book measures 9.5 inches by 8.5 inches.

2. This scale is life-sized, or 1:1, because 1 inch on your paper is the same as 1 inch measured around the book. It can be written on a scale bar (in inches or in cm), like this:

book

half size

full size

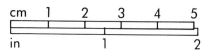

| cm | 1 | 2 | 3 | 4 | 5 |
| in | | 1 | | | 2 |

3. The darker blue paper is half the size of the first sheet. Can you draw an outline of your book at half its real size? The scale of your new "map" will be 1:2. It could be written on a scale bar like this:

| cm | 2 | 4 | 6 | 8 | 10 |
| in | | 2 | | | 4 |

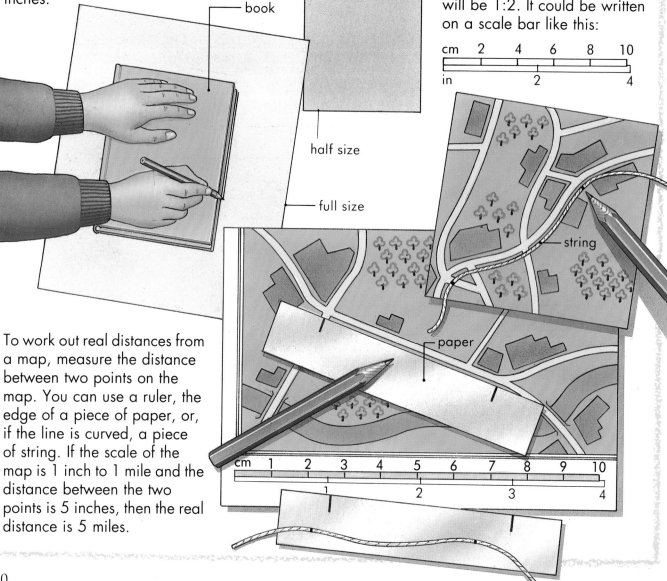

string

paper

To work out real distances from a map, measure the distance between two points on the map. You can use a ruler, the edge of a piece of paper, or, if the line is curved, a piece of string. If the scale of the map is 1 inch to 1 mile and the distance between the two points is 5 inches, then the real distance is 5 miles.

| cm | 1 | 2 | 3 | 4 | 5 | 6 | 7 | 8 | 9 | 10 |
| | | 1 | | 2 | | | 3 | | | 4 |

Symbols and Colors

Mapmakers use symbols or signs on maps so that they can give plenty of information in a small space. On the map below, for example, the pictures clearly show where there are mountains and forests. Most maps have a list called a key or a legend to tell you what the different symbols mean. There are no rules about how colors must be used on maps, but mapmakers usually use the same colors for the same things. Water is mostly blue, for example, and forests are green.

Do it yourself

tree
parking lot
freeway
telephone
road

building
water
railroad
fields
lake

Try making up your own map symbols. They should be simple and remind us of the features they stand for.

United Kingdom

M1 or A6(M)   motorway

m   ancient monument or historic building

Λ   campsite

France

autoroute

▪Mon!   monument   ⅋ ruin

(o)   campsite

United States

(80)   interstate highway

state monument, memorial, or historic site

state park with campsite

The symbols shown here are from real maps. They vary slightly in different countries.

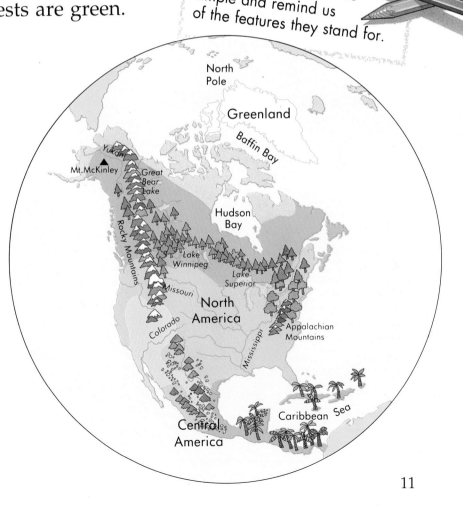

North Pole

Greenland

Baffin Bay

Yukon
Mt. McKinley
Great Bear Lake
Hudson Bay
Rocky Mountains
Lake Winnipeg
Lake Superior
Missouri
North America
Colorado
Appalachian Mountains
Mississippi
Central America
Caribbean Sea

Heights and Slopes

Mapmakers use colors and lines to show the height of the land and how steeply it rises and falls. Heights and depths on a map are measured above and below the average level of the sea. For example, when we say that Mount Everest – the world's tallest mountain – is 29,028 feet (8,848 meters) high, we mean that its height measures 29,028 feet above sea level.

 Eye-Spy

In stores, clothes are often color-coded to help us find our size quickly.

Colors for Height

These drawings show how the hills and valleys that we see in the countryside can be simplified into flat maps. First, an area is divided into sections or bands of different heights.

All land areas of the same height are given one color. The lowest land is usually colored yellow or green and higher land is shown in different shades of brown.

On the flat map below, it is easy to see which areas of land are higher. For example, the highest land is shown in dark brown.

Another way that we can show height on a map is by using contour lines. You can read about them on pages 14-15.

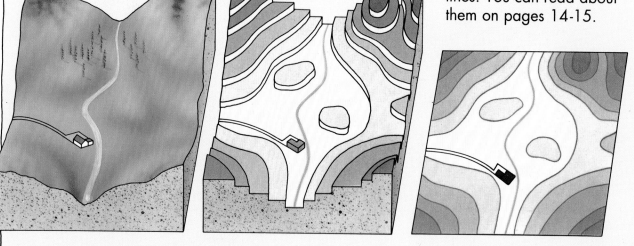

Maps that show the height of the land and other features, like rivers, are called physical or relief maps. They are often used by people who enjoy walking in the countryside.

Undersea Maps

Maps are made of the hills and valleys at the bottom of the sea, too.

Ships use sonar instruments to send sound waves down to the seabed. The time taken for the sound waves to bounce back to the ship is then measured. We know how long sound takes to travel a certain distance, so it is possible to work out the depth of the water.

On sea charts, dark blue is used for deep water and light blue for shallow water.

Contour Lines

Imaginary lines called contours are an important way of showing the rise and fall of the land on a map. Contour lines show all the places that are the same height above sea level. Contours also tell us about the slope of the land. On a steep slope, the lines are close together. On a more gentle slope, they are farther apart. If there are no contour lines, the land is almost flat.

Walkers study the contour lines on maps to find out whether hills will be easy or difficult to climb.

High Hills, Flat Maps

Here you can see how the two hills shown on the right have been mapped using contour lines.

Again, the land has been divided into colored bands according to height, but this time each band has been given a height in feet.

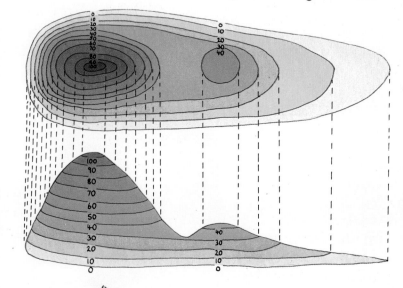

Do it yourself

Make your own contour lines to see how they work. You will need some sand or soil, a wooden board, a pencil or a sharp stick, and some yarn or string.

1. Outside, build a hill out of damp sand or soil on a wooden board.

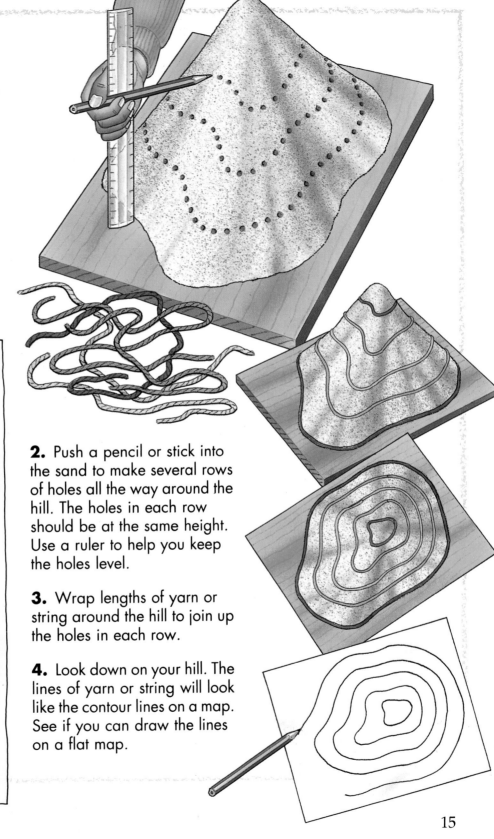

The bands or contour lines tell you that the small hill is 40 feet high and the large hill is 100 feet high. The contour lines also show you that one side of the small hill is steeper than the other.

2. Push a pencil or stick into the sand to make several rows of holes all the way around the hill. The holes in each row should be at the same height. Use a ruler to help you keep the holes level.

3. Wrap lengths of yarn or string around the hill to join up the holes in each row.

4. Look down on your hill. The lines of yarn or string will look like the contour lines on a map. See if you can draw the lines on a flat map.

15

Finding a Place

Have you ever tried to find a town or a road on a map? The easiest way is to use the map's index. This will probably give you some numbers or letters alongside the name of the place you want. These numbers and letters refer to a network of lines dividing the map into squares. The squares are called the map grid, and the numbers and letters are the grid reference. Different countries use different grids on their maps, but they usually include instructions about how to use them.

Archaeologists give each object they find a grid reference on a plan or map. This helps them to remember exactly where everything was discovered.

Finding a Building

A grid reference refers to a square on a map. It gives numbers or letters for the two lines that cross each other at the bottom lefthand corner of each square.

The reference to the lines going up and down the map (the eastings) is given first, followed by the reference to the lines going across the map (the northings). On this map, the red building is in C5 and the blue one is in I4.

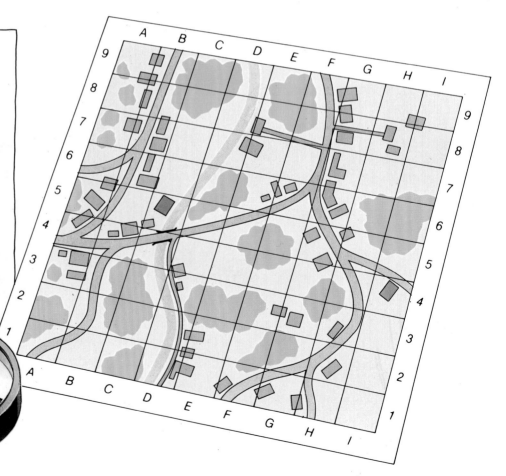

16

Do it yourself

See if you can give your friends a grid reference to explain exactly where you plan to meet them.

1. Use the map below or draw a rough map of your local park on some large-squared graph paper.

2. Label the grid squares across the top and bottom and up the sides. You can use letters or numbers or both, as on the map below.

3. Work out a meeting place. For example, the restaurant on the map below is in C8.

Giving Directions

Grid references make it easy to give directions without writing down a long list of instructions. If you can read a map, you should be able to find places without getting lost!

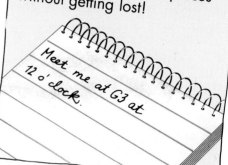

Meet me at G3 at 12 o'clock.

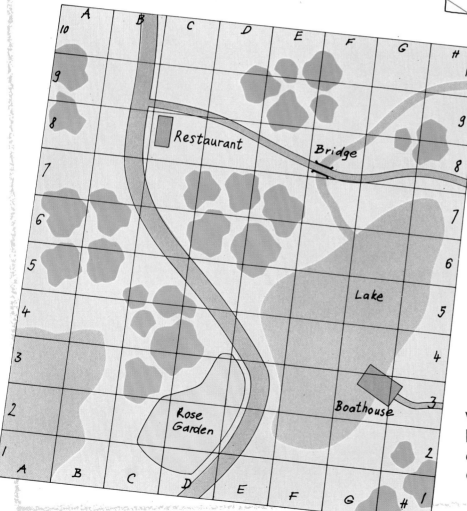

World maps also use grid lines, called lines of latitude and longitude. You can read about them on page 26.

17

Finding the Way

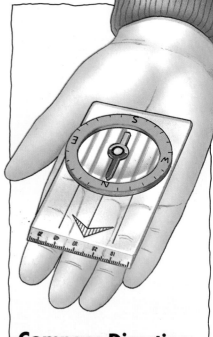

Maps do not only help us to find out where places are and the distances between them. They also tell us which direction to take in order to reach a place. In other words, they help us find the way.

Most maps are drawn with a North arrow at the top, as if you are facing North. To find out which direction North is really in, we use a compass. With a compass and a map, we can find our way in fog or even in a snow blizzard when it is hard to see where we are going.

Compass Directions

The four main points on a compass are North, South, East, and West. A compass needle is a tiny magnet that always points North.

To work out which direction to take, place a compass on the map and turn the map around until the North arrow on the map points in the same direction as the needle on the compass.

Do it yourself

Make your own compass with a magnetized needle, a slice of cork, and a shallow dish.

1. Ask an adult to help you magnetize the needle as shown below. You must stroke the magnet along the needle about 50 times.

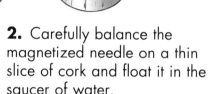

stroke the needle with the magnet in one direction only

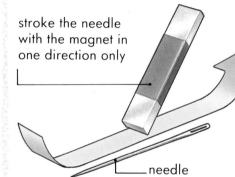

needle

slice of cork

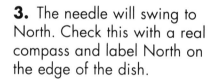

2. Carefully balance the magnetized needle on a thin slice of cork and float it in the saucer of water.

3. The needle will swing to North. Check this with a real compass and label North on the edge of the dish.

Where is North?

An arrow on a map pointing to "true north" is a straight and accurate line to the North Pole. But a compass needle always points to "magnetic north" because it is pulled by magnetic forces deep inside the Earth. Magnetic north is about 1,000 miles away from the true North Pole.

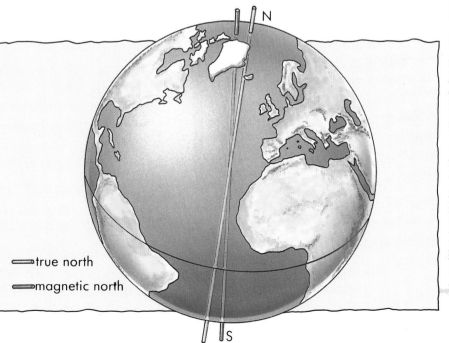

true north

magnetic north

Measuring Angles

Before they draw a map, map-makers need to know the exact position of everything to be included. To do this, the land is divided up into a network of points, and the distances and angles between the points are measured. This is called making a survey and the people who collect the information are called surveyors. To help find the angle between two points, surveyors take bearings. You can try taking a bearing using the bearing board shown below.

For hundreds of years, sailors have used sextants (which measure the angle between the Sun and the horizon) to work out their position at sea.

Do it yourself

Make a bearing board to measure an angle.

1. Ask an adult to help you make a copy of the circle shown here and extend all the lines with a ruler.

2. Label the numbers around the edge of the paper and stick the paper onto a large square board.

3. Place your bearing board on the ground. This is called your reference or base point.

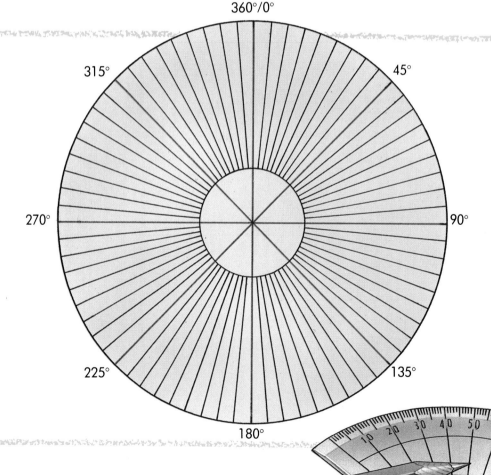

Surveyors at Work

Today, surveyors use modern electronic equipment to measure distances very accurately in just a few seconds. The instruments record how long it takes light or sound waves to travel between two points. Because we know how far light and sound travel in a certain time, it is possible to work out the distance between the two points.

4. Use a ruler to help you line up two objects you want to measure with the lines on your board. The angle between the two lines is the bearing.

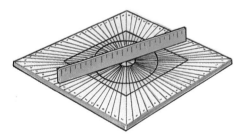

5. Read off the angle in a clockwise direction. (On this board, each space represents five degrees.)

21

Making Maps

As well as taking detailed measurements, surveyors record other information that appears on maps. This may include the type of land, such as whether it is dry or marshy, wooded or bare. Surveyors may also record the location of public buildings, like churches and schools.

Measurements taken by surveyors on the ground are backed up by photographs taken from aircraft or satellites. These photographs are called aerial photographs. They are very useful when the land is too hilly or marshy to make a ground survey.

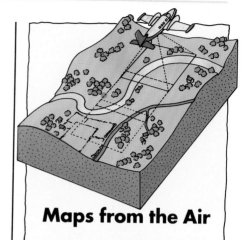

Maps from the Air

As the aircraft flies over-head, a camera takes two photographs of each section of land.

Left: Satellite photographs, like this one of San Francisco Bay, are used to make weather maps.

Below: Although maps are still drawn by hand, most map-makers now use computers.

Do it yourself

Make your own Treasure Island map!

Choose a scale for your map and draw an arrow to show the direction North. Decide how you want to show the height of the land – through colors, contour lines, or through symbols, and a key as on the map below.

You could make your map look old by crumpling up the edges and dipping the corners in tea.

Finding the Treasure

When you have finished drawing your map, add a grid and label the lines with letters and numbers.

Now decide where you are going to hide your treasure. Write some clues using grid references to guide the treasure hunters to the treasure.

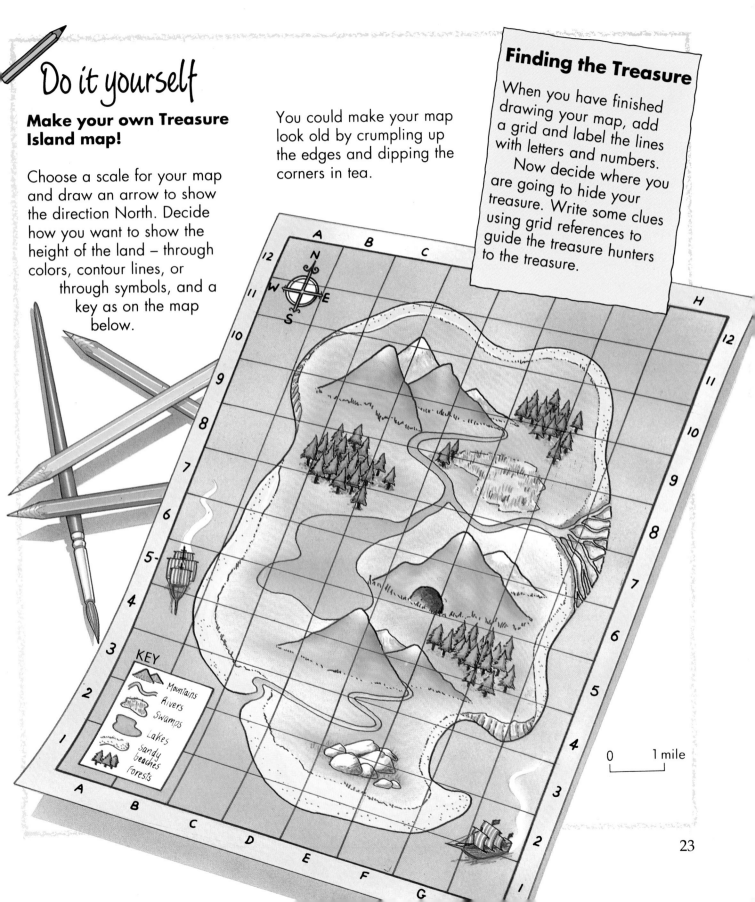

KEY

Mountains
Rivers
Swamps
Lakes
Sandy beaches
Forests

0   1 mile

23

Mapping the World

You have probably seen many flat maps of the world with the Earth's land and sea stretched out on one page or sheet. But because the Earth is round, the only really accurate map of the world is a globe – a round model of the Earth. Globes show us the true size and shape of our land and sea. They are also tilted at a slight angle because the Earth leans slightly to one side. But globes are hard to carry around. They cannot be folded up and put in a pocket like a flat map, so we use flat maps more often.

The only place that we can see the true size and shape of the world's land and oceans is in space, on satellite photographs like this one.

Do it yourself

It is not easy to make flat drawings of the Earth's surface. Some pieces of land have to be stretched and others have to be shrunk. Try making your own flat map from a globe. You will need tracing paper, a pencil, and tape.

Ask a friend to hold the globe steady while you trace around the shapes of the large land areas.

Old Maps

Hundreds of years ago most people believed that the Earth was flat, like a giant tabletop. They thought they would fall off the edge if they sailed far enough out to sea.

This map was drawn about 500 years ago. Although it is not accurate, it is easy to recognize the shapes of the different land areas. Can you recognize parts of Europe and Africa?

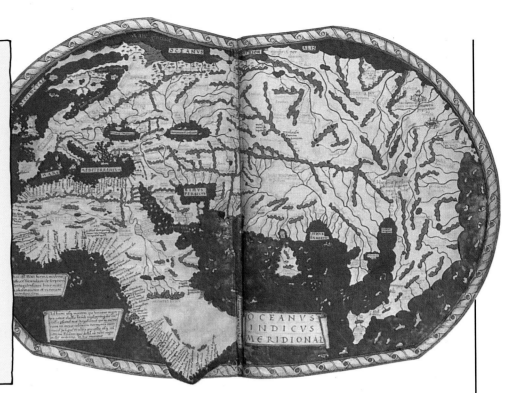

OCEANVS
INDICVS
MERIDIONAL

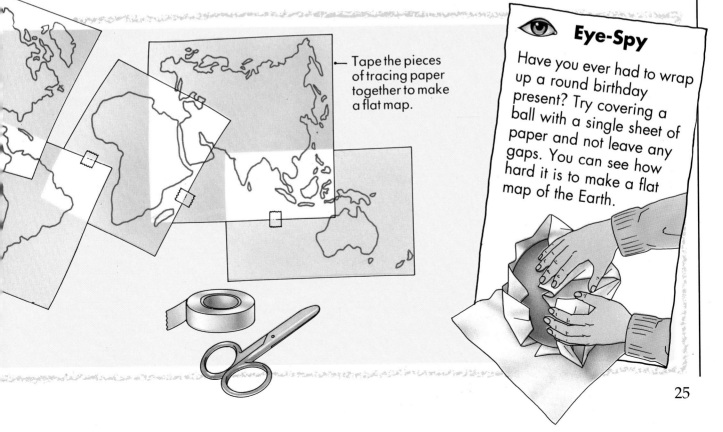

Tape the pieces of tracing paper together to make a flat map.

Eye-Spy

Have you ever had to wrap up a round birthday present? Try covering a ball with a single sheet of paper and not leave any gaps. You can see how hard it is to make a flat map of the Earth.

Latitude and Longitude

On globes and on maps showing large areas of the world, we can find a place by using a grid of imaginary lines called lines of latitude and longitude. Lines of longitude, or meridians, run up and down the map or globe. They are measured in degrees east or west of a line drawn through Greenwich, in England. Lines of latitude, or parallels, are measured in degrees north or south of the equator – an imaginary line that circles Earth's middle.

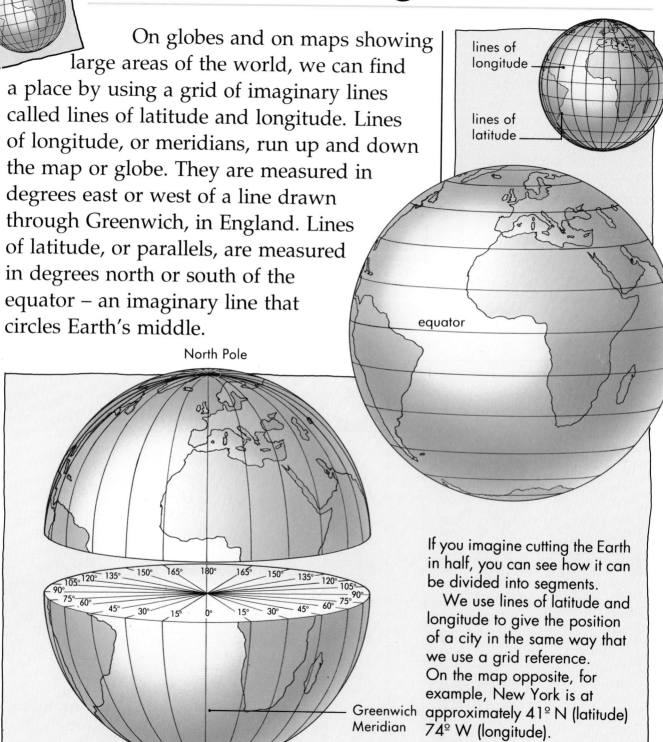

lines of longitude

lines of latitude

equator

North Pole

105° 120° 135° 150° 165° 180° 165° 150° 135° 120° 105°
90° 90°
75° 60° 75°
45° 30° 15° 0° 15° 30° 45° 60°

Greenwich Meridian

South Pole

If you imagine cutting the Earth in half, you can see how it can be divided into segments.

We use lines of latitude and longitude to give the position of a city in the same way that we use a grid reference. On the map opposite, for example, New York is at approximately 41° N (latitude) 74° W (longitude).

The Great Meridian

The 0° line of longitude can be seen as a line on the ground in Greenwich, England. It is sometimes called the Great or Prime Meridian.

Every place in the world that lies on this line has the same time, called Greenwich Mean Time, or GMT for short. Every 15° east or west of the Greenwich Meridian, the time changes. East, the time is ahead of Greenwich and west, the time is behind.

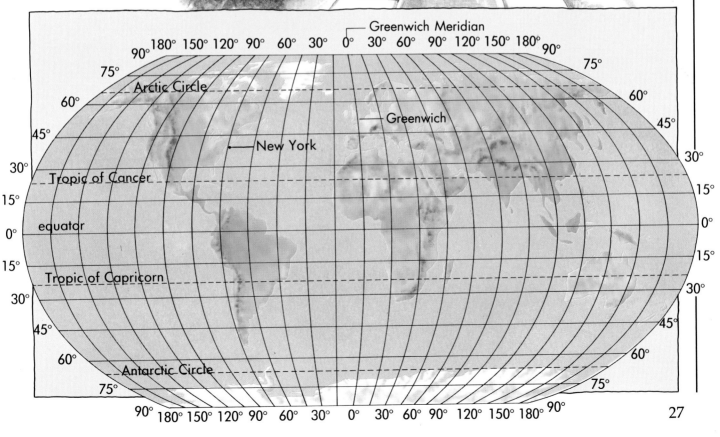

27

Map Projections

A projection is the way in which mapmakers show the curved surface of the Earth on a flat map. There are over 200 kinds of map projection, but they all distort or change the shape and size of our continents or the distances between them. This distortion is greatest on maps of the whole world. Mapmakers choose a particular map projection depending on what they need to show.

Three main kinds of map projection are shown at the top of the opposite page.

👁 Eye-Spy

Look at different atlases (books of maps) to compare the size and shape of one country in various projections. The maps above are all of Greenland. On some maps, Greenland looks bigger than South America, but South America is really eight times bigger!

Do it yourself

Try peeling an orange and making the peel lie flat. There is no way you can do this without breaking the peel.

To flatten out a world map, mapmakers may divide the land into pieces, rather like the segments of an orange.

28

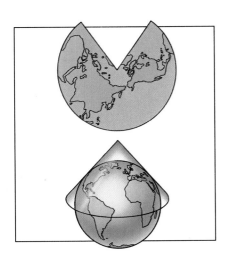

Conic Projection

This map is drawn as if a cone of paper has been placed over the globe, touching it along one line of latitude.

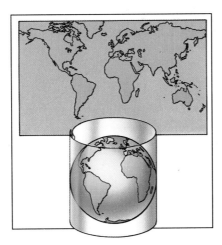

Cylindrical Projection

A cylindrical projection is made as it the globe has been wrapped in a tube, or a cylinder, of paper.

Azimuthal Projection

An azimuthal projection is made as if a flat sheet of paper touches the globe at one point in the center of the map.

The pieces are then arranged side by side and the "gaps" are filled in, or stretched, to make a flat map like the one on the right. This map is a cylindrical projection. The gray areas have all been stretched.

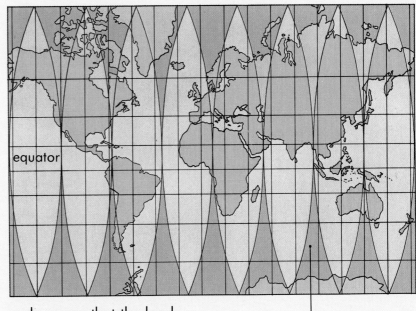

equator

stretched areas of land and sea

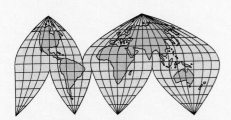

The map above is called a sinusoidal projection. Here, the globe has been cut up in

such a way that the land areas all have the correct shape and size.

Using Maps

If you look around, you will be able to see lots of different maps. Maps can show almost anything, from the number of houses in a city, or the cities in a country, to the sites of battles, the number of people in a place or the weather. Because areas change very quickly, new maps are regularly drawn with up-to-date information. See if you can find some old maps of your town in your local library. How has it changed over the years?

Now that you know more about maps, you will be able to discover how much they can tell you about our world.

Tourist Maps

Tourist maps are usually full of pictures of places to visit. They are rarely drawn to scale but they are fun and easy to use.

Maps of the Moon

Most of the maps we use are of the Earth's land and sea. But this photograph shows a map of the Moon's North Pole. It names all the craters, trenches, and valleys on the Moon's surface.

Maps like this could be used to plot the landing sites of spacecraft launched from Earth.

Mapmakers have also drawn maps of the stars in the sky, called star charts.

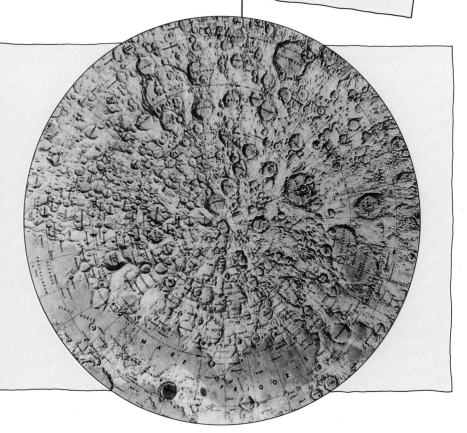

Geological Maps

Some maps show what the rocks and soil are like under the ground. They are useful in planning building work or drilling for gas or oil.

The Hiker's Code

- Always go walking with an adult.
- Tell someone where you are going and when you expect to return.
- Take a detailed map and a compass with you. A whistle is useful to call for help if you get lost or if someone is injured.
- Wherever possible, keep to the trails marked on your map.
- Take food and drink and warm, waterproof clothes.
- Take care not to leave trash, pick wildflowers, or disturb animals.

Before you set off on a walk in the countryside, study the map carefully and plan your route. Do not try to walk too far. Remember that a short distance on a map is a much longer distance on the ground!

Index

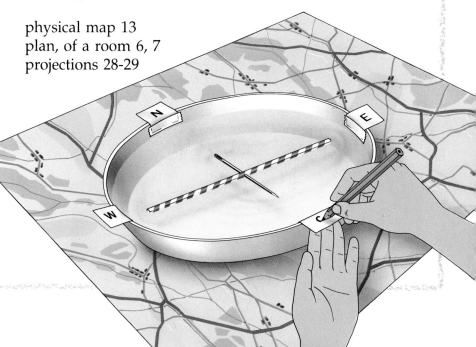